MEET POPE LEO XIV

From Chicago to the Vatican: The First American Pope

PADDY BRÉAGNAMH

PETTYFEATHER
PUBLISHING

LEGAL DISCLAIMER

CONTENTS

INTRODUCTION

Have you ever wondered what it takes to become the Pope?

Does it mean you have to be perfect? Powerful? Born into a famous family? Not even close.

This is the true story of a boy named Bobby from Chicago.

He wasn't famous or flashy. He didn't chase the spotlight. He just said yes. Yes to kindness. Yes to learning. Yes to helping others.

That boy became **Pope Leo XIV**, the leader of more than a billion Catholics around the world.

But this book isn't just about him. It's about what happens when someone listens to their heart, takes one step at a time, and leads with love.

As you read, think about the kind of world you'd like to help build—because stories like this one start with people just like you.

Let's begin.

WHO IS THE POPE, ANYWAY?

I f you've ever seen a man in white robes waving to a huge crowd from a balcony in Rome... That's probably the Pope.

But who *is* the Pope, really?

The Pope is the leader of the Roman Catholic Church, a faith followed by more than one billion people across the world. He's a spiritual guide, a teacher, and a symbol of unity for Catholics everywhere.

Some people think of the Pope as a kind of Catholic "king." But really, the Pope doesn't rule with power—he leads with service. His job is to help people grow closer to God, treat others with compassion, and care for the poor, the sick, and the forgotten.

Every Pope lives in Vatican City—a tiny country inside the city of Rome. It's the smallest country in the world, but what happens there can affect millions of lives.

When a Pope dies or steps down, something amazing happens: Cardinals from all over the world gather in a secret meeting called a **conclave**. They pray, vote, and wait for a sign—*white smoke* coming from a chimney above the Sistine Chapel. That smoke means a new Pope has been chosen.

And guess what? That happened in May 2025.

A man named **Robert Francis Prevost**—born in the United States—was just elected the new Pope. That made history.

For the first time ever, the Catholic Church chose an American-born Pope.

BUT BEFORE HE WORE WHITE ROBES OR SPOKE TO crowds in St. Peter's Square, he was just a regular boy growing up in Chicago.

And this is his story.

MEET BOBBY PREVOST

L ong before he was Pope Leo XIV, he was just **Bobby**—a regular kid growing up on the southwest side of **Chicago, Illinois**.

Bobby was born on **September 14, 1955**, into a warm and loving family. His mother, Mildred Martínez, was a librarian and active member of their local parish. His father, Robert Prevost Sr., was a U.S. Navy veteran and school administrator. They worked hard and taught their sons the importance of kindness, honesty, and faith. Bobby had two brothers, and the house was often full of energy, conversation, and the delicious smells of home-cooked meals.

The Prevost family didn't just talk about faith—they lived it. They attended Mass at St. Mary of the Assumption Church in Riverdale, Illinois, where Bobby was an altar server and sang in the children's choir. He didn't just go through the motions—he enjoyed being part of something meaningful. At home, he and his brothers would sometimes play "pretend Mass," using an ironing board as an altar and candies as communion hosts.

Even outside of church, Bobby's curiosity and kindness stood out. He loved reading and learning—maybe not a surprise, given that his mom was a librarian. At school, he asked thoughtful questions and genuinely wanted to understand how the world worked. Teachers and classmates noticed that he wasn't the loudest voice in the room, but he often had the most thoughtful one.

Bobby also showed signs of leadership early on. At St. Augustine Seminary High School, he stood out for his academic excellence and involvement. He served as editor-in-chief of the school yearbook, joined the speech and debate team, and was inducted into the National Honor Society. He was the kind of student who listened more than he spoke, but when he did speak, people listened.

One of the most important parts of his upbringing was how much the Prevost family welcomed others. They often opened their home to visiting priests and guests from their parish. These quiet, everyday moments of hospitality gave young Bobby a glimpse into the lives of clergy—and planted seeds that would one day take root.

As a teenager, Bobby started thinking seriously about what he wanted to do with his life. At first, he wasn't sure. Maybe he'd be a math teacher. Maybe he'd travel. But the more he prayed, listened, and reflected, the more he felt a quiet call toward something deeper.

One day, he sat down with his parents.

"I think I want to become a priest," he said.

There was a long pause. Then his mom smiled and said,

"If that's where your heart is leading you, follow it."

And that's exactly what Bobby did.

❧ 3 ❧
CALLED TO
SOMETHING MORE

Becoming a priest isn't something you do overnight. It takes years of studying, praying, listening, and learning. But Bobby Prevost wasn't in a hurry—he wanted to understand what it truly meant to dedicate his life to helping others.

After high school, Bobby entered college and began preparing for the priesthood. He studied philosophy, theology, and languages. He spent time in prayer and reflection. But most of all, he listened. He listened to the wisdom of teachers, to the struggles of others, and to the quiet stirrings of his own heart.

Before he became a priest, Bobby studied something that might surprise you: **mathematics**.

He earned his degree from **Villanova University**, where he loved solving tough problems, spotting patterns, and thinking logically. Math helped him understand that the world is full of mystery, structure, and beauty—just like faith.

During this time, Bobby felt drawn to a special kind of priesthood. He joined an order called the **Augustinians**, a group of men who lived in community, took vows of poverty, and focused on service, education, and simplicity. Named after Saint Augustine, one of the early thinkers of the Church, the Augustinians believed that life was best lived in love, humility, and truth.

Bobby liked that. He didn't want fancy robes or titles. He wanted to serve. He wanted to live in a way that honored people's dignity and showed the world what real love looked like.

After years of preparation, he was finally ordained a priest in **1982**. His family was there, smiling with pride. The boy from Chicago had followed his calling. But Bobby wasn't done.

While many new priests start serving in a local parish, Father Bobby was asked to do something different—something bold. The Augustinians needed priests in **Peru**, a country in South America where many people lived in poverty and had little access to the Church. They needed someone who was willing to learn a new language, live simply, and walk alongside communities in some of the poorest neighborhoods in the country.

Father Bobby said yes.

He packed his bags, hugged his family goodbye, and boarded a plane for a place he'd never been before.

He didn't go to preach from a pedestal. He went to listen. To learn. To serve.

❧ 4 ❧
LIFE IN PERU

When Father Bobby stepped off the plane in Peru in 1985, everything felt different.

The air was warm and dry. The streets buzzed with motorbikes, music, and laughter. Spanish filled the air—fast, friendly, and full of energy—and the neighborhoods were painted in bright colors that made everything feel alive.

It was beautiful. It was overwhelming. And it was exactly where he was meant to be.

Father Bobby had been sent to a small town in northern Peru called **Chulucanas**, a place where many families lived in poverty but were rich in faith and community spirit. He wasn't there to be in charge. He was there to serve—and to learn.

First, he had to learn Spanish. He practiced with teachers, neighbors, and children in the street—laughing at his own mistakes and getting better every day. But more than learning the language, he listened to people's stories. Stories of struggle and hope. Stories of hard work, strong families, and deep faith.

Life in Peru wasn't always easy. The country was facing serious challenges at the time, including violence from rebel groups. Father Bobby's church was even threatened. One night, a bomb exploded outside the chapel. But instead of leaving, he stayed. He believed that to lead meant standing with people—even when things got dangerous.

He didn't just visit Peru—he became part of it.

After a few years, Father Bobby moved to another city called **Trujillo**, where he kept helping wherever he was needed. He taught future priests, visited sick families, and even traveled by horseback to reach small villages where people had never seen a priest before.

He wasn't afraid to get his hands dirty—literally. When flooding hit the area, he waded through muddy water to bring food and comfort to people who had lost everything. When refugees from Venezuela arrived with nothing but the clothes on their backs, he helped them find shelter, jobs, and dignity.

People called him "**Padre Roberto**"—and they loved him.

He didn't try to act like he had all the answers. He didn't show off. He just kept showing up—with a gentle heart, steady hands, and a deep love for the people around him. Some even started calling him **"the Saint of the North."**

He stayed in Peru for nearly twenty years. Two decades of walking with the poor, praying with the sick, building up communities, and reminding people—through words and action —that they mattered.

When it was finally time for him to leave, many wept—not because he was powerful, but because he had loved them well.

❧ 5 ❧

A HUMBLE LEADER

After nearly two decades in Peru, Padre Roberto had become more than just a local priest. He was a trusted leader—someone people turned to in times of joy and sorrow, celebration and crisis.

Word of his quiet strength and thoughtful leadership began to spread. And in 2004, he was given a new mission: he was asked to return to the United States to lead the **Augustinian Order worldwide**.

It was a huge responsibility. The Order had priests in dozens of countries, each with their own challenges and communities. Father Bobby didn't want power or recognition—but he said yes because he believed in serving where he was needed most.

He moved to Rome and took on the role of **Prior General**, which meant he helped guide Augustinians around the world. He listened to their stories. He encouraged them in their missions. And he reminded them of their purpose: to live simply, love deeply, and serve humbly.

For **twelve years**, he traveled to countries like Nigeria, the Philippines, Italy, and the Democratic Republic of Congo— wherever his fellow Augustinians needed support. He spoke many languages, but always with the same tone: kind, calm, and full of respect.

Even in this important position, Father Bobby never changed. He still made time to visit the sick, eat meals with everyday people, and pray quietly in the back of chapels. He didn't need a spotlight—he just wanted to do what was right.

Then, in 2014, Pope Francis noticed something. He saw that Robert Prevost was the kind of leader the Church needed more of: thoughtful, faithful, and full of heart.

So Pope Francis appointed him a **bishop** in a city called **Chiclayo**, back in northern Peru. Bishop Prevost returned joyfully to serve once again among the people who had become like family.

But his journey wasn't over yet.

In 2023, Pope Francis brought him to **Rome** to help with the Vatican's most important offices. Just one year later, he was made a **cardinal**—a trusted advisor to the Pope and one of the men eligible to help choose the next one.

He didn't know it yet, but he wouldn't just help *choose* the next Pope.

He would *become* him.

✤ 6 ✤

HOW POPES ARE CHOSEN

C hoosing a new Pope isn't like voting for class president. There are no campaign posters, no speeches, and definitely no commercials. It's a process filled with prayer, tradition, and a little bit of mystery.

When a Pope dies or steps down, the Catholic Church must

choose someone new to take his place. That job falls to a group called the **College of Cardinals**—around 130 senior leaders from around the world.

They gather in **Vatican City** for a secret meeting called a **conclave**, which takes place inside the famous **Sistine Chapel**—the one with the beautiful ceiling painted by Michelangelo.

Once inside, the doors are locked. No phones. No internet. No reporters. Just the cardinals, their prayers, and their votes.

Here's how it works:

- Each cardinal writes down the name of the person they believe should be the next Pope.

- The votes are counted.

- If no one receives at least **two-thirds of the votes**, they vote again.

- They keep voting—sometimes for days—until they agree.

When a decision is finally made, something dramatic happens. A small chimney on the roof of the chapel releases a puff of smoke.

If the smoke is black, it means: *no Pope yet.* If the smoke is **white**, it means: *we have a new Pope!*

Crowds gather in **St. Peter's Square**, staring up at the chimney, waiting for the signal. Bells ring. Cameras flash. Excitement spreads around the globe.

And then, a cardinal appears on a balcony and says the famous Latin words:

"Habemus Papam!"

(*We have a Pope!*)

That's what happened on **May 8, 2025**.

The cardinals had chosen a humble man from Chicago. A

man who had served the poor in Peru, led with gentleness, and never expected to wear the white robes himself.

That man was **Cardinal Robert Francis Prevost**.

And when he stepped onto the balcony, he had a new name: **Pope Leo the Fourteenth.**

❀ 7 ❀

INTRODUCING POPE LEO XIV

T he world held its breath.
    Thousands of people stood shoulder to shoulder in
St. Peter's Square, their eyes fixed on a small balcony
above. Some were praying, some were crying, and some were Face-
Timing their grandmothers.

When the balcony doors opened, the cheers were deafening.

Out stepped a man in white robes—gentle-eyed, steady, and maybe just a little surprised to be there. Cardinal Robert Francis Prevost had just been elected the **267th Pope of the Roman Catholic Church**.

But he wasn't "Cardinal Prevost" anymore.

He had chosen a new name: **Pope Leo XIV**.

WHY LEO?

Popes don't keep their old names—they choose new ones to signal the kind of leader they hope to be. By choosing the name "Leo," he was following in the footsteps of some strong and faithful Popes from the past.

One of the most famous was **Pope Leo I**, who stood up to invading armies and helped protect the Church during a time of chaos. He was known for his courage, his wisdom, and his big heart.

By choosing the name "Leo," Pope Robert sent a quiet message:

"I want to be a shepherd who protects the flock. I want to lead with strength, but also with love."

THE FIRST AMERICAN POPE

The crowd that cheered in St. Peter's Square wasn't just excited—they were witnessing history. Pope Leo XIV was the **first American-born Pope ever**.

People from the United States, Peru, and beyond rejoiced. News stations buzzed with headlines like:

"From Chicago to the Vatican!"

"Humble Priest Becomes Pope!"

"Padre Roberto is Now Pope Leo!"

But those who knew him weren't surprised.

He had spent his life helping the poor, walking with refugees, building churches in remote villages, and leading with a calm, steady voice. He had never chased attention—and yet, here he was, standing at the center of the Catholic world.

HIS FIRST WORDS

Pope Leo's first words as Pope weren't loud or dramatic. He didn't shout. He didn't make big promises.

He simply looked out at the sea of people and said:

"Peace be with you."

And the crowd went quiet.

In that moment, people didn't just see a Pope. They saw a person. Someone who was humble. Someone who listened. Someone who cared.

A POPE WHO WALKS WITH THE PEOPLE

In the first weeks of his papacy, Pope Leo XIV did something remarkable: **he kept being himself**.

He refused a fancy apartment and chose to live simply. He asked for plain white papal robes, without the extra gold trim. He visited a home for refugees in Rome and asked to meet the kitchen staff. He made time for children, the elderly, and those who often go unseen.

He told reporters he hoped to "walk with the people—not above them."

In one of his first speeches, he said:

"The Church must always choose the path of humility, listening, and hope."

He spoke often about caring for the poor, protecting the planet, and listening to young people. He reminded everyone that faith isn't about power—it's about presence.

A BEGINNING, NOT AN ENDING

Being elected Pope wasn't the finish line for Bobby from Chicago —it was just another "yes."

Yes to serving.

Yes to listening.

Yes to walking with love.

In those early weeks, people from all over the world—especially Latin America and the U.S.—felt hope. Maybe this Pope would bring a fresh perspective. Maybe this moment was a reminder that anyone, from anywhere, could be called to something big.

But Pope Leo XIV didn't act like a man with a grand plan.

He acted like someone who still believed in the quiet power of showing up, staying humble, and doing the next right thing.

❧ 8 ☙
WHAT WILL YOU DO?

L ittle Bobby from Chicago didn't set out to become Pope.

He didn't dream of standing on balconies or having crowds cheer his name. He simply followed one small "yes" at a time—saying yes to helping others, yes to learning, yes to leading with love. And look where that yes led him. From the streets of Chicago to the villages of Peru, to the heart of the Vatican.

But Pope Leo would be the first to say: **This story isn't just about him.**

It's about you, too. You don't need to wear white robes or speak five languages to make a difference. You can start with what you already have.

A kind heart.

A curious mind.

A willingness to do what's right—even when it's hard.

You can notice who's sitting alone at lunch. You can ask questions that others are afraid to ask. You can be the person who listens when no one else does. That's what Bobby did. Over and over. For decades. He never tried to be famous. He just tried to be **faithful**.

As his papacy begins, many people around the world hope that Pope Leo XIV will continue to walk with the poor, listen to the young, and lead with quiet courage—just like he always has.

So, what will *you* do?

Will you follow your calling?

Will you lead with love?

Will you say yes to the people who need you?

Because maybe—just maybe—your small yes today could change the world tomorrow.

REFLECTION QUESTIONS

1. What surprised you the most about Pope Leo XIV's life? Why?
2. Pope Leo studied math before becoming a priest. What does that tell you about how our talents can serve in different ways?
3. How do you think living in Peru helped shape the kind of leader Pope Leo XIV became?
4. What part of Pope Leo's story inspired you the most?
5. If you could ask Pope Leo XIV one question, what would it be?

TIMELINE OF KEY MOMENTS

1955
Robert Francis Prevost is born in Chicago, Illinois

1970s
Begins studies for the priesthood
Studies mathematics at Villanova University

1982
Ordained as a Catholic priest

1985–2004
Serves as a missionary in Peru

2004
Becomes Prior General of the Augustinian Order (based in Rome)

2014
Appointed Bishop of Chiclayo, Peru

2023

Called to the Vatican to serve in the Roman Curia

2024

Made a Cardinal by Pope Francis

May 2025

Elected as **Pope Leo XIV**, the 267th Pope in Catholic history

GLOSSARY

Augustinians – A religious order of Catholic priests and brothers who live in community and focus on service, inspired by the teachings of Saint Augustine.

Bishop – A senior leader in the Catholic Church who oversees a group of churches in a region, called a diocese.

Cardinal – A high-ranking Church official who advises the Pope and helps elect a new one when needed.

Conclave – A private meeting where cardinals gather to elect a new Pope.

Missionary – A person who travels to share faith and help others, often in communities with limited resources.

Papal Name – A new name chosen by a Pope when elected, often to honor a past Pope or saint.

Pope – The spiritual leader of the Catholic Church, also known as the Bishop of Rome.

Vatican City – The smallest independent country in the world and home of the Pope and the central offices of the Catholic Church.

Villanova University – A Catholic university in Pennsylvania where Robert Prevost studied mathematics before becoming a priest.

White Smoke – A traditional sign that appears after a successful Papal election.

AUTHOR'S NOTE

As a parent, educator, and lifelong learner, I believe the lives of faith leaders should feel both inspiring *and* accessible to young readers. When Cardinal Robert Francis Prevost was chosen as **Pope Leo XIV**, I saw an opportunity to share a modern story of humility, service, and leadership with children around the world.

This book isn't just a biography—it's an invitation. I hope it sparks conversations about kindness, courage, and calling. I hope it helps kids see that great leaders don't have to be loud or brash. Sometimes, they're simply the ones who listen well and love deeply.

— Paddy Bréagnamh

MINI SAINTS & MISSIONARIES
LIBRARY SERIES

Discover more true stories of faith and courage!

The ***Mini Saints & Missionaries Library*** brings the lives of saints and missionaries from around the world to young readers in a way that is inspiring, relatable, and full of joy.

Each book shows that sainthood isn't about being perfect—it's about trusting God, loving boldly, and living each day with courage. See other titles in the Mini Saints Library below.

Blessed Carlo Acutis: The Boy Who Showed the World Jesus

Carlo Acutis loved soccer, video games, and technology. But more than anything, he loved Jesus—and he showed the world that even ordinary life can be extraordinary when lived with love. Follow Carlo's journey from a lively boy in Italy to a global witness of faith, hope, and joy. **Paperback & e-book available on Amazon.**

———

Saint Joan of Arc: The Girl Who Heard God's Call

Joan was just a farm girl in France when she began hearing God's voice calling her to lead. With faith in her heart and armor on her shoulders, she answered that call—riding into battle to defend her people. Discover the true story of the teenage saint who followed God with fearless devotion. **Paperback & e-book available on Amazon.**

———

Saint Lorenzo Ruiz: The Brave Witness of Manila

Lorenzo Ruiz grew up in the busy streets of Manila, dreaming of a simple, faithful life. But when trouble came, he made a courageous choice that would lead him across the sea—and into the arms of God. Follow the true story of the first Filipino saint. **Paperback & e-book available on Amazon.**

———

Venerable Augustus Tolton: Priest of Freedom

Meet Venerable Augustus Tolton, the first Black Catholic priest in the United States—and a hero of faith and courage. From his daring escape to freedom as a boy, to his ordination in Rome, to building a welcoming church in Chicago, Augustus never gave up on God's call—even when others shut the door. **Paperback & e-book available on Amazon. Free audiobook included!**

———

Saint Thomas the Apostle: From Doubt to Devotion

Follow Doubting Thomas from the dusty roads of Galilee to the tropical shores of India—where he became one of the earliest and bravest Christian missionaries. The first in our upcoming Mini Saints sub-series on the Apostles. **Paperback & e-book available on Amazon.**

———

Saint Patrick: The Boy Who Forgave

Patrick lived a quiet life near the sea—until he was taken from his home and carried across the water as a captive. Alone in a strange land, he learned to pray, to listen, and to forgive. Discover the true story of the saint whose forgiveness changed a nation. **Paperback & e-book available on Amazon.**

———

What Saints, Blessed, & Venerables do you want to see next? **Scan the QR code or visit pettyfeatherpublishing.com/minisaints** to learn more about the series, join our mailing list and share your suggestions!

JOIN THE MINI SAINTS CLUB
GET PRINTABLE BONUS ACTIVITIES!

When you sign up for the **Mini Saints Club**, you'll get exclusive extras to help kids grow in faith, joy, and kindness—just like Saint Carlo Acutis. Sign up now to get the first printable bonuses, sent straight to your inbox.

———

Carlo Coloring Page

Bring Carlo's story to life with your own colors and creativity.

Carlo's Clicks of Kindness 7-Day Challenge

A week of simple, tech-positive acts of kindness to spread light online and off!

———

Join Our Mailing List to download your free bonuses at: **www. pettyfeatherpublishing.com/saintcarlobonus**
(or scan the QR code on the previous page).

www.ingramcontent.com/pod-product-compliance
Lightning Source LLC
Chambersburg PA
CBHW070652130626
46555CB00006B/2845